BUMPER
STICKER
RELIGION

BUMPER STICKER RELIGION

Seven Messages Unstuck From Bumper Stickers

BY CARL B. RIFE

C.S.S. Publishing Co., Inc.
Lima, Ohio

Scripture quotations are from the *New Revised Standard Version of the Bible*, copyright 1989 by the Division of Christian Education of the National Council of the Churches of Christ in the USA. Used by permission.

9320 / ISBN 1-55673-600-2 PRINTED IN U.S.A.

To my family — Judy, Mark and Stephen — who keep my feet on the ground as they encourage me to greater heights.

Table Of Contents

Foreword

The idea for this sermon series came to me when I was driving into a bank parking lot and saw a car with a bumper sticker that read "Let My Kids Pray." That bumper sticker began an internal dialogue in me that ended up with my putting a note on the windshield of that car. The note said: "Who's stopping them?"

It occurred to me that religious bumper stickers would be a good jumping off point for sermons. They are something we see every day and to which we have myriad reactions. So I started looking for more bumper stickers and had my church members do the same.

The sermons are sometimes an elaboration, sometimes a correction, sometimes an argument, sometimes a discussion of the particular sentiment found on the bumper sticker. I have attempted to throw light from the Christian faith on the particular subject that is generated by the bumper sticker.

Through the use of the bumper stickers I was able to touch in my sermons a number of the basic Christian themes such as creation, the second coming, prayer, forgiveness, God's Word, grace and discipleship.

I am particularly grateful to the good people of Milford Mill Church to whom these sermons were first preached. Their response to the first couple of sermons encouraged me to pursue the bumper sticker sermon series. Some of the material in the book reflects discussions I had with members following the preaching of the sermons.

I am also deeply indebted to my church secretary Phyllis Skovran for her transcribing of the rough manuscript from the audio tapes of the sermon and for her daily help and encouragement in my ministry.

Carl B. Rife

Honk, If You Love Jesus

John 14:15; 13:4-35

"If you love me, you will keep my commandments.
— John 14:15

In the film *Dead Poets' Society,* the teacher, Mr. Keating, jumps up on a desk and then invites all of his students to do the same. It was a very effective teaching device because it helped his students to see life from a different angle, from a different perspective even in the classroom. It was his way of dramatizing that if you keep looking at the same things in the same way you will miss some important things in life. You will even miss life itself.

What I would like to suggest is that we look at the messages of religious bumper stickers the next couple of weeks.

13

It is my way of having you jump on a desk to see religion and life from a different angle. I would like us to examine the phrases, the cliches, the half-truths of the religious messages on the bumper stickers people sometimes display on their automobiles. Today the bumper sticker is "Honk, If You Love Jesus."

Twice as I told people that I was going to preach a sermon on this bumper sticker they told me true stories. A friend of mine told a story about his colleague who happened to be a United Methodist district superintendent, a black United Methodist district superintendent. This man was driving down the road and he came to a light where the car in front of him had this bumper sticker, "Honk, If You Love Jesus." He said, "The thought went through my mind: 'I love Jesus; why shouldn't I honk?' " So he honked his horn and the person in the car set race relations back a couple centuries with his provocative response.

Then last night I again shared the fact with some of our friends that I was going to preach on this bumper sticker. They told me a similar story. They came to an intersection and there was a car in front of them that had a sign "Honk, If You Love Jesus." They thought, "Well, we love Jesus" and so they honked. This time it was a gesture that was shared, not words. Need I say anymore?

Now I think it is clear that if we are going to display our faith so boldly, if we are going to advertise our beliefs so boldly on our cars or any other place, then our lives better be consistent with the faith that we claim. If we really love Jesus, we will live according to the pattern set forth in his life.

Did you hear the scripture this morning? It does not say, "Honk, If You Love Jesus." It says, "If you love me, [if you love Jesus], keep my commandments, [keep the commandments of Jesus]." If you read elsewhere in the Book of John, the central commandment of Jesus is that you "love one another as I have loved you." To love according to Jesus' pattern is to love, in other words, with the same kind of love that Jesus shows to us and has shown to his disciples. It is a costly

14

kind of love that goes beyond the limits we normally set for our kind of love.

Now the next statements are the most important part of the sermon. If you really love Jesus, you will realize how much our merely honking about Jesus and our faith turns other people off. If you love Jesus, you will realize how much our merely honking about Jesus and our faith turns other people off. If you love Jesus, keep his commandment. In other words, "Love, if you love Jesus" is the message. Just making noise, just honking about our faith has a terribly negative effect on others at the edge of the chruch and outside the church.

The thing that concerns me most as a pastor in the church is the realization that the church often gets in the way of its message. Our noise about our faith, our honking about Jesus is seen by others to be at odds with the pattern of our lives. It is so easy, it is so very easy for others to pick this up and to be turned off. We need to lower our decibels and raise our discipleship. Our lives need to proclaim what we profess with our lips.

Somewhere along the line I came across the saying that, "Your life screams so loud I can't hear what you are saying." I say to you as forcefully as I can, unless we begin to live according to the pattern of Jesus' life, all our noise as a church will not make any difference in the world. The world is waiting for us to set a pattern that speaks loudly and clearly. Not by honking, but by living.

The most effective communication of our faith is the way we live our faith. This is a poem I'm sure most of you have heard and the central part of this poem says it clearly:

We are the only Bible the careless world will read.
We are the sinner's gospel; we are the scoffer's creed;
We are the Lord's last message, given in deed and word;
What if the type is crooked? What if the print is blurred?

Someone recently described to me another person in the church as giving the Lord "heart-service" seven days a week,

15

not just "lip-service" on Sunday. In the language of the sermon: we are called to give Jesus "heart-service," not "honk-service." We are called to live our faith, not just make noise about it. We are called to live according to the pattern of love set forth in Jesus' life.

Let Our Kids Pray

Matthew 6:6; 26:36-44

But whenever you pray, go into your room and shut
the door and pray to your Father who is in secret;
and your Father who sees in secret will reward you.
— Matthew 6:6

Quite a few years ago I saw a bumper sticker on a car that
said, "Let Our Kids Pray." I had an immediate reaction and
I acted immediately on the reaction. I went to my car and got
a pen and paper and wrote on the paper "Who's stopping
them?" and put it under the windshield wiper.

Now that bumper sticker and my response get us into
the whole area of prayer in the public schools. I would like
to preface everything I have to say this morning with the

understanding that committed Christians can differ on this issue. The apostle Paul in his writings in one place speaks about a word from the Lord where he is certain that he is speaking God's Word to the people. Then in other places he admits that it is his committed opinion. What I am sharing with you this morning is not a direct word from the Lord but my committed opinion.

I think the place we need to begin is with an understanding of what prayer is. Prayer is that intensely personal, intimate conversation with God. There are several theological assumptions caught up in this understanding. First, there is a God to whom to pray. Further, this God is no less than personal, perhaps supra-personal whatever that means, but no less than personal. This God is the One at the heart of the universe who can listen, who does hear, who does respond to our prayers. Now this is a faith assumption about God and about prayer. It is based on the solid ground of scriptures and the experience of countless Christians down through the ages.

The writer of Matthew talks about prayer best being done in private or in the closet where one speaks from the deepest part of one's being to the deepest part of the universe. I believe that the best model for prayer is what you heard read this morning in scripture, Jesus' prayer in the Garden of Gethsemane. It is not like our formal prayers, our spoken prayers in church, as important as those kinds of prayers may be. It is that intensely personal conversation, that intensely personal wrestling that Jesus does in the hour of his greatest need.

Jesus' prayer is a real prayer, the opening up of his entire life, that surrendering of his being to the one he called Father, or more precisely Daddy. That kind of prayer depends upon a context of faith, a community of faith. Again I say prayer grows out of a faith understanding that is a by-product of a community of faith such as the church, and not the public sector such as the public schools.

The second thing that needs to be said about this whole matter is that it is not the state's role to teach prayer. I have heard some people say that we need to bring God into our classrooms. Every time I have gone anywhere in a secular setting and have been asked to give the invocation, I have never invited God to be present because I believe God to be there already. Our responsibility is to open our eyes and see the presence of God wherever we are. This God does not need to be brought into a classroom. God is already there. We need to help our young people have the eyes that can see God at work, in the classroom, or wherever they are.

Let our kids pray. When I stop to think about it, no teacher ever stopped me from praying. There was many a test when the only hope I thought I had was to reach out to God in prayer. Of course part of God's answer was "Why didn't you pray to me earlier and I would have given you the answer, and that is 'Study'?" When you take that by extension, no teacher can stop a child from praying. No authority anywhere on this earth can stop another human being from praying.

Now the kind of prayer we are talking about when we talk about prayer in the public schools would be a prayer so formulated not to offend anybody. It would be a prayer developed by a committee that would be then revised by another committee until we would have this pale, anemic reflection of what prayer is all about. It is nothing like that intense personal prayer that we find Jesus praying in Gethsemane.

Some say well, prayer even in a formal, watered-down prayer cannot hurt anyone. I say that takes away the entire meaning of prayer when it is viewed that way. What we want our kids to do is to learn how to pray the kind of prayer that Jesus prayed in Gethsemane. Not give them some official version of a prayer that gets official approval through many committees.

That leads to the third thing: The whole area of the doctrine of the separation of church and state. I said this before but I think it's important to be clear about it. There are legitimate spheres of activity for the church and religion and legimate spheres of activity for the state. A part of the great insight and understanding of our founding fathers was to keep a tension between these two spheres: the sphere of the church and the sphere of the state; the sphere of faith and morality and the sphere of welfare and well-being of the people. The important thing about keeping tension between these two is that it keeps us from the abuse and tyranny of one or the other spheres.

The church reserves the right to speak to the state and to call it into question when it operates in a way that runs alien to the values of the faith. But the church has also experienced this corruption down through the years. In this situation the state needs to confront the church with its corruption.

If you study the history of civilization you know how dangerous it can be when religion gets mixed up with the state and you cannot distinguish at all between the two. I'll give you two cases: one was the inquisition when the state carried out the wishes of the church in trying and torturing those seen to be heretics. The most recent one was Iran under the leadership of the Ayatollah Khomeni where religion, the church and the state were blended into one with no check on one by the other.

So you see it's with this kind of understanding that I have just shared with you that I say in response to the bumper sticker "Let Our Kids Pray." Who in the world is stopping them? For prayer is a reflex of our deepest being to turn toward God, a spiritual tropism, and no one, no one anywhere can stop anyone from doing just that. Let us remember, when we think of prayer in the public school, not to think of the pale, anemic, watered-down official version of prayer that some official might write to satisfy everybody. Rather let us think of our young people out of their experience in the church and home being able at any moment to live out their lives in prayer reflection on the presence of God in their midst and how God can be a vital part of their lives.

So that is the answer to the bumper sticker, clear and simple, "Let Our Kids Pray." If we have done our job, in the home and the church, who is stopping them?

God Made My Day

Psalm 118:24

This is the day that the Lord has
made;
let us rejoice and be glad in
it.
— Psalm 118:24

"God Made My Day" is one 'anonymous Christian's response to the infamous line of Clint Eastwood's Dirty Harry character who says, "Go ahead, make my day," as he holds a gun on a thug and dares him to make a move. The implication is that Harry Callahan's day would be made if he were given the opportunity by a false move by his antagonist to mete out his rough version of justice by wasting the guy, as the language in these movies goes.

21

Over against this cynical view of life is this affirmation on a bumper sticker that some people have placed on their cars, "God Made My Day." And what I would like us to do this morning is to try to understand this phrase and to see in what sense can we affirm that God made our day.

We can say that God made our day in the sense that God creates all days. That is a faith perspective and that faith perspective leads to a way of approaching life. If we really believe at the very core of our being that God is the creator and the Lord of all time, of all days, it would affect our attitude toward life, toward each day. The Psalmist exclaimed, "This is the day that the Lord has made, let us rejoice and be glad in it." I saw a poster sometime ago with a little boy sitting in a high chair with a bowl of spaghetti over his head and it said, "This is the day that the Lord has made, let us rejoice and be glad in it." You know there is a real message in that; we can rejoice even in those days when the kid puts spaghetti over his head.

One commentator said that "life is one damnned thing after another." That is not the view of the Psalmist at all. Each day, says the Psalmist, is a gift from God. Each day is an opportunity to rejoice, to appreciate the gift of life. Not long ago I attended a seminar for clergy and the leader got up in front of the group and said, "This is the day that the Lord has made, don't blow it." Could we wake up in the morning and say that? This is the day that the Lord has made, don't blow it. I like that very much. This is a day laden with opportunities, a day to live, to love, to serve, a day to create, a day to celebrate. Don't blow it.

Granting that what I said is true, we still face the challenges of each day. There is another bumper sticker I did not dare to use in this series. It says something like "stuff happens!" It is crude and vulgar and cynical. It also speaks to a truth about life. The point is, that each day that we face is not a day ready made to bring us happiness. Stuff happens, terrible stuff, stuff that makes it hard to believe that this is the day that the Lord has made. The testimony of scripture and faith is that God will give us the strength to face the stuff, the challenges of each day.

I really never appreciated the story of the Israelites in the wilderness and their receiving manna from God: the fact that at the end of each day they could not store up manna for it would rot and they would have to wait again for the next day to receive new manna. As I was studying the Lord's Prayer, the person who was commenting on this prayer pointed out that the phrase "give us this day our daily bread" is connected with that experience of manna in the wilderness. The point being this, behind manna, behind daily bread is God's grace, God's strength. And God does not give it to us in abundance that we can store it up for the future. When we look at our lives, at what we are facing today and what we are facing tomorrow and down the line, we would like to know that we will be able to cope with whatever comes our way. What we receive is strength for the day, manna, daily bread.

And that underscores the promise, perhaps the most significant promise of scripture. I am aware of this promise because my pastor during my formative years would constantly say in every opportunity he had to share: "There is one promise that we can depend on and that is the promise that God made through Christ that his grace will be sufficient." He was constantly preaching about sufficient grace. The phrase comes from Paul who said that the Lord assured him in the midst of his affliction that "My grace is sufficient for you (2 Corinthians 12:9)." Now one of the things that I have experienced since I have heard that message is that sometimes it seems we get pretty close to the edge and sometimes it is a close call, but God's grace is still sufficient.

Like the old television program we need to approach life "One Day At A Time." We need to face the challenges of each day with God's help and explore its opportunities. It is possible to move beyond merely surviving the day to thriving.

There is another dimension. Not only can we say that God made my day in the sense that God creates all days. Not only can we say that God made my day in the sense that God gives

23

us the strength to meet the challenges of each day, but we also have to say that God made our day in the sense that God shows that the way to make our day is to help make somebody else's day. True joy and happiness come when we take our gaze off our own problems and redirect our attention and energies to others. One reason our problems loom so large is that when we put our gaze on our problems they become magnified by our self-concern. One thing that the medical world is discovering is that through our attitudes and through what we do, we release all kinds of chemicals in our systems, some negative and some positive. And one way to insure our continued problems is to gaze inward. A kind of acid begins to eat away inside us when we do that. Literally, not just figuratively, an acid begins to eat away at our being.

A couple of weeks ago my son Stephen and I stumbled on to this whole experience of making somebody else's day that we did not expect. We had planned for the summer to take some small trips to go see all the minor league teams in the Orioles organization play so that some day we could say, "We've been there and saw that guy when he was down in Class A, Double A, Triple A." So we decided to go up to Frederick and we had some time before the game. We went to visit a fellow named Teddy who is in his 80s and who became a friend of mine when we lived in Frederick. Teddy came from Germany as a teenager, learned to be a chef and became the head chef at the Francis Scott Key Hotel in Frederick. At 80-some years old, he is bent over with arthritis and having lost his second wife a couple of years ago, he is a very lonely man. We stopped by to see him and were sharing with him that we were on our way to McCurdy Field to see the Frederick Keys play. I am absolutely convinced that it was some kind of inspiration from God because I never thought that he would do it. I said, "Teddy would you like to go out and eat supper and then go to the game?" And Teddy brightened up and said, "Sure I'll go." We went out to eat and then we went to the game. At the game many people came up and talked to Teddy because practically everybody in Frederick knows Teddy.

The thing that Stephen and I both commented on almost simultaneously was that what really made our day was that somehow, even somewhat by accident, we had helped to make somebody else's day. And what a difference it made; it at least doubled our joy of going to the game.

You see that what I am saying is God made life so that when we help to make somebody else's day it helps to make ours. It is so obviously clear, that I do not know why we get caught up in the dead-end of our own worlds, in our own problems and are not able to see that truth.

I think the phrase "God Made My Day" is a vast improvement over Dirty Harry's statement "Go ahead, make my day," which would simply give him the satisfaction of blotting out another life and feeling that maybe he had contributed in a small way to justice in the world by that act. Whereas when we say the phrase "God Made My Day" what we are really voicing is a statement of faith about whom is behind it all, about whom is behind it all, about who gives us the strength, the grace sufficient to meet each day, and about who made life so that when we reach out to others we begin to find what God intends us to have all along, fullness of life. This is the day that the Lord has made; let us rejoice and be glad!

Christians Aren't Perfect; They Are Forgiven

2 Corinthians 5:18-19

All this is from God, who reconciled us to himself through Christ, and has given us the ministry of reconciliation; that is, in Christ God was reconciling the world to himself, not counting their trespasses against them, and entrusting the message of reconciliation to us.

— 2 Corinthians 5:18-19

There it was on a bumper sticker — "Christians Are Not Perfect; They Are Forgiven." My theological mind worked on that for a while and part of me applauded the modesty of that particular insight. A part of me realized that like many things compressed in just a few words, it was a half truth, an inadequate statement about the whole issue of forgiveness.

This morning as we look at this bumper sticker "Christians Aren't Perfect; They Are Forgiven," I would like us to take a closer look at this matter of forgiveness.

Forgiveness is the act of reaching out to another who has done wrong to us to reestablish a broken relationship. I think the important part of this understanding of forgiveness is the part about the restoration of a broken relationship. Because when you stop to think about our broken relationships, it is very seldom that there is a totally guilty party and a totally innocent party. Very seldom is there one who needs to forgive and one who needs to be forgiven. It is a lot more clumsy, complex matter than that. Usually both participate in the guilt of the broken relationship. It is true that in the brokenness somebody has to initiate the reaching out for the restoration of a relationship and begin the process of healing. Eventually both partners have to reach out to the other.

There are four things that I would like to say about forgiveness now that we have established a basic understanding of what forgiveness is.

The first is that forgiveness is crucial to human life because brokenness is endemic to our experience. I have noticed how easy it is to go through life and everything seems to be going all right. Then when you never intend it to happen, something does happen and a relationship is broken. Our life just does not work the way it was meant to work when we experience brokenness and need forgiveness. Our health is affected, our work efficiency suffers, even our relationship with other persons outside the broken relationship deteriorates.

I know over the last couple of weeks in speaking with several members of this church, that they have experienced this brokenness in their own lives. They know how crucial it is for them to find some kind of restoration, some kind of healing for their situation.

28

We experience this broken relationship in at least three dimensions: our relationship to God, our relationship to other; our relationship to ourselves. Even then you cannot so neatly divide these three dimensions of our brokenness and our need for restoration. They all flow into one another and through one another and when we need restoration it is at all three levels or dimensions. Forgiveness is absolutely crucial to life.

The second thing about forgiveness is that forgiveness is central to the Christian faith. When we talk about God's love, there is that aspect of God's love that is always seeking to overcome brokenness both between God and ourselves and between ourselves and others and even within ourselves. There are many different words used in the Old and the New Testament to talk about forgiveness. The witness is clearly there that God is working to bring healing, to restore broken relationships. According to the witness of the scriptures and the witness of Christ, forgiveness is rooted in the very nature of God. "God was in Christ reconciling the world to himself (2 Corinthians 5:19)."

You heard in the children's sermon this morning that God is love. One very important aspect of that love is that part that seeks to restore broken relationships.

The third thing that needs to be said about forgiveness is that God's forgiveness extends to all human beings. I want to make this clear. I want to make this perfectly clear, because this gets to the heart of the sermon. It is at this point where I begin to disagree with the bumper sticker. God's love is universal. God's forgiveness reaches out to every person despite their faith. God's desire is to reach out to every human being on this earth with the forgiveness that restores relationships.

So if I were writing that bumper sticker I would at least start out by saying not that, "Christians aren't perfect; they are forgiven, but that "Human beings aren't perfect; they are forgiven." In our need for forgiveness we stand with all of humanity; in the offering of forgiveness we stand with all of humanity.

That leads to the fourth thing to be said: Christians know and accept that forgiveness and extend it to others. Christians are in on an open secret and I underscore the word open. It is not to be a closed-shop type of thing. God's love and forgiveness is for all. Persons do not have to repeat the creed the way we repeat it, or believe the way we believe for God's forgiveness to be a part of their life. They just have to be aware of it, and then accept it. For in all attempts to establish restoration, a person has to be willing to allow that to happen.

Then the crucial part comes. Forgiveness needs to be extended to others. You see forgiveness becomes real first when it is appropriated, taken in, when it is really accepted. In addition, forgiveness becomes real only when it is extended to others. Someone once put it this way. In order for God to give me forgiveness, he has to come across a bridge. This is a bridge over which I have a measure of control. If I keep destroying that bridge in my relationship to others, there is no bridge there for God to cross to grant me forgiveness. It is not that God does not want to forgive us or that God will only forgive us on a tit for tat basis. God cannot forgive us when our broken bridge or bitterness prevents it.

As I was thinking about this, I came across a story about a pastor named Peter Miller during the Revolutionary War. He was a very beloved pastor in his community. There was one person, however, who hated Pastor Miller and abused him in every way he could. Now it happens that Peter Miller discovered that this man was a traitor to his country and was tried and convicted of treason and was to be executed. The trial was in Philadelphia and Peter Miller took off from Ephrata by foot. He arrived just in time to talk to General Washington and say that he would like to have this man freed of charges so that he would not be executed. General Washington said, "I cannot do this for your friend." Peter Miller said, "My friend? That man is probably the worst enemy I have in the world." George Washington said, "That being the case, that changes everything. I give him a pardon." Peter Miller had walked 60 miles to get this pardon, but he wasn't finished because the execution was taking place 15 miles away. When he walked to that place he got there just at the time that they were arriving at the gallows. And as Peter Miller's enemy saw him coming he said, "Here comes Peter Miller. He came all the way from Ephrata to be able to have the last laugh as I am executed." Peter Miller turned over the papers to him for his freedom. Peter Miller knew something about God's forgiveness and knew that it only becomes real when we extend it to others.

I would like this morning to rewrite that bumper sticker. It would go like this: "Humans aren't perfect, they are forgiven; Christians know and accept that forgiveness and extend it to others." The only problem is those bumper stickers are not big enough to handle that kind of message. But our lives are!

God Said It. I Accept It.
That Settles It.

2 Timothy 3:16-17

All scripture is inspired by God and is useful for teaching, for reproof, for correction, and for training in righteousness, so that everyone who belongs to God may be proficient, equipped for every good work.

— 2 Timothy 3:16-17

Like the other bumper stickers we talked about, this bumper sticker raises some issues for us. The meaning of this bumper sticker greatly depends on the spirit in which it is shared.

For some, this bumper sticker expresses an arrogant and rigid feeling that they have a corner on God's Word. How

33

they understand God's word is how everyone else should understand it to the last detail.

For others, this bumper sticker expresses a different approach. These people know that while they do not understand God's Word in every detail, they do understand the most important thing that God is trying to say to us through the scriptures: God loves and cares for us deeply.

How to understand God's Word in the scriptures is an important issue. This issue has caused great controversy and even sharp division in some denominations. I believe it is more important to immerse oneself concretely in the scriptures to hear God's Word than it is to give assent to some proposition about the scriptures such as the infallibility or inerrancy of the scriptures.

The task of discovering God's Word in the words of scripture is of crucial importance. John Wesley, the founder of the Methodist Church, pointed to a way of working out this task with his quadrilaterals. While his quadrilaterals go beyond the task of interpreting scripture to discerning God's truth in a larger context, they can be helpfully applied in this area also.

Scripture according to Wesley is the primary source of God's revelation to us. We should in no way diminish this primacy. The scriptures are a record of God's revelation and human response to that revelation. God uses that crystallized record to break through repeatedly to us to communicate his will and way. "As we immerse ourselves in the biblical testimony, as we open our minds and hearts to the Word of God through the words of persons inspired by the Holy Spirit, faith is born and nourished, our understanding deepens and develops, and both are the core of faith and the range of our theological [understanding] are expanded and developed" ("Our Theological Task" in the *The Book of Discipline* of the United Methodist Church).

Tradition is the ongoing understanding and interpretation by the community of faith of the original revelation. When we sit down to read scripture we are not without a great cloud of witnesses who share with us their insights and understandings

34

of the text. What an accumulation of insights and understandings! We have a rich heritage from which to draw much wisdom on how to interpret the scripture. It is the height of self-centeredness and arrogance to ignore this rich fellowship of believers who surround us when we read and study scripture.

Experience is the personal appropriation of the truth of God's unmeasured mercy one discovers in scripture. In *The Book Of Discipline* of the United Methodist Church in the section titled "Our Theological Task" the writer states the truth this way, "There is a radical distinction between intellectual assent to the message of the Bible and doctrinal propositions set forth in creeds, and the personal experience of God's pardoning and healing love." Scripture does not become real for us until we personally appropriate its message. To claim the truth of scripture and not to live its message greatly blurs its truth.

Reason is the use of the God-given gift of mind to discern the truths of God's revelation. When we read and interpret scripture we cannot set aside the full use of our reasoning powers. Reason is a gift of God to be used in God's service. Reason, however, is not an end in itself and should not be made the ultimate criterion. We need to recognize that revelation and experience may transcend the scope of reason.

Used together in openness to God's Spirit we can discover God's Word for us in the words of scripture. For Christians God's Word is most clearly spoken in the person of Jesus Christ. Martin Luther called Jesus the Living Word. And the clear word that God has spoken in Jesus Christ is that God loves us utterly and unconditionally. We may not know all the details of scripture or we may disagree on interpretation of scripture with others. This much we know: God loves us. God has shown us this love in Jesus Christ. And we are to love others with this same kind of love.

When interpreted this way then I can agree with the statement, "God said it. I accept it. That settles it."

I Found It!

Luke 15

"Or what woman having ten silver coins, if she loses one of them, does not light a lamp, sweep the house, and search carefully until she finds it? When she has found it, she calls together her friends and neighbors, saying, 'Rejoice with me, for I have found the coin that I had lost.' Just so, I tell you, there is joy in the presence of the angels of God over one sinner who repents."

— Luke 15:8-10

For those of you who may have not been here during this series on bumper sticker religion and for others who need a reminder, what I have been doing is using some religious bumper stickers as a take-off point for my sermons. More pericisely I have been using these bumper stickers as a beginning point to talk, if I could, with the persons who displayed them on their cars. Today's bumper sticker is "I Found It." That doesn't say a whole lot by itself. Although I am sure we can read into it, if it's a religious bumper sticker, that it has something to do with finding faith and with finding God.

As I thought about this bumper sticker it reminded me of something that used to be in magazines. There was a question above a picture that said, "What's wrong with this picture?" The question this morning is what is wrong with this bumper sticker "I Found It?" The question is who is looking for whom. If I wanted to end the sermon right now, the whole gist of this sermon is that the bumper sticker really does not have it right — "I Found It." The bumper sticker really ought to say, "God Found Me."

Now since we have some more time I would like to elaborate on that phrase "God Found Me." I would like to elaborate by asking several questions.

The first question is, "Who Is Lost?" It is not God who is lost according to the New Testament; it is human beings who are lost. In the 15th chapter of Luke, Jesus talks about many ways in which human beings get lost.

One is like the sheep that never intends to get lost but nibbles its way blade by blade of grass until it gets away from the rest of the flock. The shepherd then has to go out and bring that sheep back to the flock.

Or we can get lost more like the story of the woman who loses the coin. It is an accident; it is not anything that is planned; it happens.

Or lostness can come like in the story of the Prodigal Son. It can come from a very intentional decision to turn from one's source of being. It can come from a very intentional choice to distance oneself from one's source of life.

I think at times when we talk about lostness we forget that there are a variety of ways of getting lost. My suspicion is that most of us in the church get lost by one of the first ways, by nibbling our ways from the source of our life or by some accidents along the way that lead to our lostness. Although there are times when some of us do make some intentional choices in which we are not consciously aware of our underlying decision to cut ourselves off from the locus of our life and being.

Who is lost? It reminds me of a story of a husband and wife who had been married for 15 years and the wife is sitting buckled in on her side of the car and the husband is sitting buckled in on his side of the car. The wife says, "Dear, why don't we sit as close as we used to?" The husband turns and says to her, "Well, honey, who moved?" Why isn't God as close to us as he used to be? The question is, "who moved?" Who is lost? The first thing we find wrong with this bumper sticker is that what we are looking for is not lost. God has not moved; God is not lost. We are the ones who get lost.

The second question is, "Who does the seeking and the finding?" As I have studied world religions and all types of modern day efforts to find meaning in life, to find that something more, to find that something extra that will make all the difference in life, the one thing that I have found unique about the Jewish and Christian traditions is that the understanding of God is of a God who is a seeking God, a God who is like the shepherd who goes out looking for the lost sheep, or like the woman looking for the lost coin. Even in the story of the prodigal son the father runs to meet the son who has realized his lostness and is coming down the path to home.

I majored in philosophy in college. One thing I discovered was that in an attempt to be intellectually respectable, God got turned into an impersonal being or force. God became an "it" in most philosophical systems. One thing that helped me more than anything else was to understand that God is personal and is not an "it." Such a view holds its weight intellectually because the highest thing we know on the human level is human personality. If that is the highest thing we know, then God can be no less than that, God cannot be an "it." God is at least like a person. Some have gotten around the problem by saying God is suprapersonal. However you put it, God is personal, God is one who feels and moves toward us in his love. That leads to one other statement about who does the seeking and finding.

This morning we sang "Amazing Grace." Grace expresses the faith understanding that God's love seeks and moves toward us even before we do any seeking or reaching out to God. Grace is the faith understanding that even if we are unworthy, God reaches out to us. If God waited to reach out to us until we were worthy, or till we made the move, God might never have the opportunity to move. The very heart of the Christian message is that God in his fullness addresses us personally in Jesus Christ. He entered into our life seeking to bring us the message of his love, his care. God is a seeking, personal God; he moves toward us in grace.

That leads to one last question. "What is our role if God moves toward us and we are lost?" I have to back up and take a running start on this answer. There was a man by the name of Soren Kierkegaard, a Danish philosopher back in the 19th century. The interesting thing is that his writings did not make a real impact on thought and religion until our century. In some of his writings he talks about several different steps that we as human beings take in the religious quest.

The first level he talks about is the aesthetic level. Now you do not have to worry about the technical name. Just trust me that the first level is called the aesthetic level. What he talks about is that in this level people dabble in life, trying to enjoy its pleasures. The key word of this level is pleasure seeking.

The second level of life is the ethical level. That is when people begin to take life seriously and the issues of life seriously and give themselves to seeking the good.

The first level pleasure, the second level the good. The first level casual dabbling, the second level earnest living. The third level, he says, is divided into two and he calls them Religion One and Religion Two. Religion One has to do with what we were talking about in this bumper sticker where we seek the truth, where we yearn, where we reach out to find this

40

something extra we know is somehow a part of life. That is Religion One and the emphasis there is on truth. So you go pleasure, good, truth.

But he said there is another level that we have discovered. This level is revealed in the scriptures. This level is Religion Two where the whole thing is turned around and the grace of God seeks us. The word here is trust. What we can do at this level is to respond in trust to the God who has already moved toward us. To let go and to let God.

My younger son is trying to learn how to swim and he cannot understand how you can float on water. The interesting thing about floating is that it is an act of faith. That water will hold you up if you let go and trust it to do so. If you don't, you are going to sink. In fact, sometimes the more you thrash around the quicker you will sink. It is much the same with the faith in God at this second level that Kierkegaard is talking about. Not to work so hard in seeking pleasure or the good or truth but to let go and let the God who is seeking you in the first place embrace you in his love. It makes all the difference in the world.

Indeed what happens when you look back over your own seeking, over your own yearning for God, is that one thing you will discover is that God was a very big part of that seeking and that yearning. If someone comes and talks to me and says, "Pastor, I can't find God, I have this need, I want to find God but I can't find God." I say, "You are extremely close to the kingdom because the very yearning, the very seeking you are sharing with me is God already at work in your life. You let go and let God pull you up in his love and faith."

Warning!
In Case Of Rapture
This Car Will Be Unmanned

Mark 13:14-37

"From the fig tree learn its lesson: as soon as its branch becomes tender and puts forth its leaves, you know that summer is near. So also, when you see these things taking place, you know that he is near, at the very gates. Truly I tell you, this generation will not pass away until all these things have taken place. Heaven and earth will pass away, but my words will not pass away.

— Mark 13:28-31

During recent weeks we have been using some religious statements that are found on bumper stickers. We are using those sayings as the occasion to agree, disagree, correct, add, subtract, to understand more deeply our faith. Today we tackle a really big one. It says, "Warning! In Case Of Rature This Car Will Be Unmanned." And immediately when I shared the words of this bumper sticker with my wife she said, "I know a correction: this car will be unwomanned or unpersonned."

I think it may be helpful to talk about something we do not talk a lot about in the church. There are some things you need to know. There is some language we use that we are not familiar with, for instance the word rapture. The word rapture refers to the belief associated with the second coming of Jesus. It is a belief that believers will be caught up into the clouds and transported directly to heaven. If you cannot quite understand what that is all about, all you have to do is watch Star Trek, when they say, "Beam me up, Scotty." That is a kind of rapture, a transporting up. Paul uses that language in 2 Thessalonians: "We shall be caught up together with them in the clouds to meet the Lord in the air."

Then there is the whole doctrine of the second coming in which the rapture is a part in at least some people's belief. It is the belief that Christ will physically return to earth at the end of the present age and set everything straight. Now let me share with you that as I was growing up I was not excited, enthused or enamored in any way about the idea of a second coming. It scared me to death. I literally had dreams and nightmares about it. I do not really believe my parents or anyone else in the world knew that it bothered me. I had dreams at night that the Lord returned and returned with a cosmic kind of fireworks display that scared me to death. So as a result as I was growing up, in my study in Sunday school and church and later in seminary, I put that whole thing on the back burner. I believe we cannot do that. I think we have to take a fresh look at this whole doctrine of the second coming.

I would like to do it by doing it in three main chunks. I really have to simplify but at least trust me that when I

44

simplify that I do know it is a little more complex than this. I will paint the big picture.

Let us look first at what the New Testament has to say on this matter of the second coming. You cannot read the gospels, the letters of Paul, some other epistles, the Book of Revelation without realizing that the overwhelming message of the New Testament is that of the imminent return of Jesus and the imminent embarking of God's reign on earth. Now not all of that written by the different writers agree in all the details and with their descriptions. But the overwhelming message is that Jesus will return and God's kingdom will be restored within the lifetime of those who lived with, saw, and heard Jesus.

The other thing you notice when you read these stories about the second coming is that the language describes this event in very poetic, enigmatic, and sometimes troubling imagery called apocalyptic. It was in existence before Jesus was here on earth; he used some of that language to talk about himself. It is a language that is troubling, it is not easy to understand, and sometimes it is even difficult to accept.

One other important thing that we should note is that obviously the imminent return of Jesus did not take place in the lifetime of the early believers. Therefore the church was left with a problem of how to respond to the reality of something that Jesus said was going to take place, something that Paul said was going to take place and something that the writer of Revelation of John said was going to take place, but did not take place in the lifetime of Paul and John.

It is interesting that there has been a whole variety of responses down through the ages in dealing with this failure of the imminent return of Jesus. One response was that God's kingdom was equated with the church. Therefore the people believed that as the church gained in control and influence, God's kingdom thus made inroads in the world. That is the way that God would bring about his kingdom.

Sometimes the church forgot or completely ignored the teaching of the second coming. Since the teaching was mistaken in the sense that it did not happen exactly as predicted, therefore one could say that you could put it aside and just ignore it.

The other response was that from time to time there would be groups of believers that would rediscover the doctrine of the second coming in the New Testament. They would lift up that message and emphasize it. These were called Millenial Groups. They knew that there was something that was missing in the interpretation of the Christian faith and they tried to bring that truth to the fore. They reinterpreted the second coming to speak to their situation. It is interesting that the conditions about which Jesus speaks in the book of Mark could have been understood as applying to the various situations down through the ages in which believers found themselves. Wars and rumors of wars and all the other things that happened have been conditions that believers in any age could look at and say that the time is right for Jesus to return.

Another response of some people was a more secular outlook that developed over the years that as human beings made progress, that progress was equated with the spread of God's kingdom. That view was particularly prevalent at the end of last century and beginning of this century. Then we saw that so-called kingdom human progress is not always steadily in the right direction. It is hard to make a case that we are steadily progressing toward God's kingdom.

In some cases there was another response that is woven through all the responses and that is the belief that Jesus had already returned in the life of the Spirit. If you read the Gospel of John, you find that this is a belief that in some sense God's return in Jesus might be understood to be through the Spirit.

Now after we said all of this about what is in the New Testament and examined some responses to the message of the second coming down through the age, the real question is: Where are we now? We cannot ignore or mute the teaching about the second coming. It is too much a part of the New Testament. It is too much a part of our historic creeds. It is too much a part of our liturgy to cross it out and just go with what remains. So the question this morning is: What does the message of the second coming have to do with us today? Let me share with you a few of the main themes.

The doctrine of the second coming teaches that God will bring to completion in Christ what God has begun in Christ. I think all of us realize that even with all that God accomplished in Christ there is still unfinished business in our world. And God has been working through the Spirit with us to bring that work to consummation. The doctrine of the second coming says there is a goal out there, there is a point at which God will bring it all to fruition.

Now God is the initiating agent of human redemption. God initiates. Humans respond. This being clearly understood, and this has to be clearly understood, I point out that our Christian faith teaches that humans have an important part to play in the whole matter of God's purpose for creation. God shares responsibility for his creation with human beings. All the talk about the second coming should never take away our responsibility in the here and the now for caring for all of creation and sharing God's message, the message of redemption.

Further, we do not need to know the details or believe in a certain version of the second coming. I think this is where we have gotten hung up in the past. The version that I got as a child, that scared me to death, is not really what the second coming is all about. The second coming is something to anticipate, not something to fear. You see what I was afraid of was the version that the Jesus of the second coming was absolutely, utterly different from the Jesus of the first coming. When I understood how God works, then I knew that what God will do in Jesus in the second coming will correspond to how he has acted in Jesus in the first coming. We do not need to know the time or the manner God will bring history to completion. In the Gospel of Mark, Jesus says, "Even the Son is not let in on that part of God's plan."

Our responsibility is to be faithful now. To be faithful and to live in the hope that our efforts to follow Christ and his way of life are not in vain. That is what the doctrine of the second coming is all about. If we live according to the way that God has shown us in Jesus Christ, those efforts will not be wasted. The good that we do will be caught up in that consummation and will contribute to that consummation. It makes all the difference to know whether we are going about doing good or we are just going about. God has a purpose and we are to be faithful to that purpose now no matter if there is a second coming within our lifetime, within the next generation or 2,000 years from now. We are to live in expectation that God's way revealed to us in Christ will ultimately triumph. We can contribute to that by our faithfulness.

So I would say to you this morning that the teaching of the second coming should neither be ignored or be blown out of proportion with exotic language that is not consistent with the Christian gospel. We as Christians should all hope and work for the day when God will fully bring about the way of life in the world that God revealed to us in Jesus Christ.

www.ingramcontent.com/pod-product-compliance
Lightning Source LLC
Chambersburg PA
CBHW060936050426
42453CB00009B/1029